A Pocket Guide to Total Representation (TR)

How to achieve simple and effective electoral reform of the House of Commons and the House of Lords

GW00393906

A POCKET GUIDE TO TOTAL REPRESENTATION (TR)

How to achieve simple and effective electoral reform of the House of Commons and the House of Lords

3rd Edition

Aharon Nathan

With grateful thanks to my son Michael whose unstinting encouragement and help in getting this and other books and articles published, has ensured my ideas will survive me.

CONTENTS

INTRODUCTION

Over the course of the last 4 years our political institutions spent all their time and effort on Brexit. For better or worse this is now behind us and, putting party politics aside, the result of the last election has finally provided political stability, call it a truce, for at least the next 4 years. There is much for us to deal with, not least the new Covid-19 crises, however we should also use this period to urgently review the functioning of our political institutions and find solutions that can repair the damage and dysfunction that the chaos of the Brexit process revealed.

Our Constituency based Parliamentary Democracy, I believe, still remains the best political system to enable all our citizens to be represented and to participate in the political process. But as with any such system it needs to be overhauled from time to time and updated when new situations arise. Since the Glorious Revolution, unlike and in contrast to our Continental neighbours across the Channel, we have followed a practical and evolutionary path to constitutional changes, facilitated by the absence of a rigid written Constitution.

This absence of a codified written Constitution has allowed us, over the years, to create quasi constitutional arrangements that made our legislation flexible and facilitated smooth changes that preserved the cohesion of our social and political frameworks. This was matched by the freedom of our courts to create and accept legal precedents based on equity rather than on written rigid dictates which helped to render our judicial framework flexible and adaptable.

The combination of these concepts of practicality, tempered by inherent equity and fairness, has helped, in the main, to resolve our political conflicts. Nothing typifies this better than the way Reform Acts were debated and enacted in Parliament, reflecting and accommodating the political conditions and evolving social conflicts of the time. And the pressure for such changes generally came from the bottom up, from the people and their elected constituency MPs in Parliament. This healthy real democracy has been threatened in recent times by the rise of the evolving power of the Political Parties, enforced by the Whips; a process that has impaired the independence of the Constituency MPs as the guardians of the will of the people.

The alien concept of referenda – first in the form of the Scottish Referendum and then the Brexit Referendum – has been a further blow on our form of Parliamentary representative democracy. Instead of bringing voters together they tore into the fabric of our political and social cohesion.

But most of all our democracy has been harmed by the justified belief of so many citizens that their vote is wasted, that there is no point in voting at all because in many constituencies their vote will not make a difference, and that their voice is not being heard and does not count.

So four years on from the Brexit referendum with a return to Binary Politics, the Conservatives have been busy using their majority in Parliament to consolidate the UK's independence from the EU under Prime Minister Boris Johnson (albeit at time of writing currently curtailed due to Covid-19). It is therefore not surprising that the calls for change are now coming from the ranks of a revitalised Labour party under Sir Kier Starmer. Disillusionment in politics has started to give way to a revived desire to re-examine how to steer politics through its next phase; and as a result Electoral Reform is back on the political agenda.

In 2011, the Liberal-Democrats, in coalition with the Conservatives, put the AV system to a referendum. It was a missed opportunity since AV had no chance of winning support and it looked like the chance of achieving electoral reform had been lost for a generation. But that was before Brexit and this new revived opportunity must not be squandered a second time.

There are of course a multitude of electoral systems all vying for attention, but there is only one system that meets the current challenges facing the country and that is Total Representation or TR. As this short book explains, it fuses an element of sorely needed Proportional Representation into our present First-Past-the-Post system whilst still retaining the all important link of MPs to their Constituencies; and most importantly it operates by the busy voter placing one cross on a simple ballot in exactly the same way that is done today.

The system is summarised in the first chapter and then the following two chapters go on to explain in more detail how it can be applied to revitalise the House of Commons and re-activate the House of Lords.

By way of background I have also included in two appendices my essays on Referendums (written on the 31st August 2016) and on the Binary of our Politics (written on the 20th April 2018). Both essays appeared at the time on my website www.aharonnathan.com

This Pocket Guide draws heavily on two books which explain in more detail the origin and working of TR and its implication for Parliament. These books, available from Amazon and high street bookshops are:

"The crisis in our Democracy", (ISBN 978-154-311089-0) written with Andrew Edwards in 2017,

The other is: "Fixing our Broken Democracy, The Case for TR" by Dr Ken Ritchie (ISBN 978-147-828695-0) published in 2012.

Professor Tony Wright, who as a Labour MP chaired for over a decade the select committee on Reform of the House of Commons (which was referred to as the "Wright Committee") wrote the foreword to Dr. Ritchie's book. In it he wrote: *".....this book by Ken Ritchie is so welcome and timely. It makes the case for what he calls Total Representation, which combines the single member constituency system with an imaginative (and flexible) way to get additional members from the best losers. It is not necessary to sign up to the precise details of such a system to recognise that it makes an important and un-dogmatic contribution to thinking about what a desirable kind of electoral system might look like. It deserves to be widely read, and discussed. I hope it will generate the kind of informed debate on the issue that is now so badly – and urgently – needed."*

He wrote this in 2012. If, as he put it, electoral reform was badly and urgently needed then, it is clearly needed all the more urgently today.

Aharon Nathan BLitt
Wimbledon, April, 2020

CHAPTER 1

A BRIEF SUMMARY OF TOTAL REPRESENTATION (TR)

TR, Total Representation is a simplified variant of the Single Transferable Vote. It preserves the Westminster model of FPTP and infuses it with a dose of PR to ensure a greater representation of the electorate. TR's appeal is in the way it carries out reform of the First-Past-The-Post electoral system with minimum upheaval. Its distinctive feature is the way it gives weight to the votes of unsuccessful candidates and brings fairness into the electoral process.

TR needs one ballot paper with one vote. It is simple to operate and less confusing to the voter than other competing systems like AV or AMS. TR requires all candidates (including those competing in Party Lists) to start off by running in the constituencies. It does not require long list ballot papers which mix party allegiances and confuse the busy citizen in the voting booth.

The PR element of TR gives an active role and leverage to the runner-ups in the constituencies by keeping their hopes alive in between elections even in "safe seats". Thus TR converts the rival runner-ups into vigilant watch-dogs, monitoring the incumbent MPs and guaranteeing their constant accountability.

How TR works

TR is a **constituency-based** system. For it to work properly, constituencies need to have a similar number of voters each to **avoid *gerrymandering*.** The majority of seats in parliament (say 80%) will be awarded to the winners of these races, just as they are under the Westminster system today.

So each party puts up candidates for election in the constituencies. Their names appear on the ballot paper in alphabetical order and next to each name is the party he or she represents. However, these candidates also appear on their own party's national "list" of all its candidates headed by the party leader.

Voters go to the polls and put a **cross** against their preferred local candidate. Whoever wins a simple majority of the votes becomes that Constituency's Member of Parliament (CMP) – again, just like today.

From then on, the innovations begin. All the "successful" ballots drop out. So if you voted for candidate X and candidate X wins, your ballot is judged to have already secured representation. As for the **"unsuccessful" ballots** (for example, if you voted for candidate Y, but candidate Y did not win in your constituency) these are placed in a **giant nationwide pool** – and it is from these that the remaining seats (20% for example) are decided using the PR method and awarded to the various parties to select Party Members of Parliament (PMPs)

These remaining seats are allocated proportionally amongst the parties according to a quota of a minimum number of required votes per seat. This is reached by dividing the number of "unsuccessful" votes by the number of the remaining seats. Obviously in, for example, an 80/20 FPTP/PR system as recommended here t**he legitimacy and the status of the PMP is assured** by the fact that he needs often 3 to 5 times as many party voters countrywide to be elected as that needed by the CMP in the constituency.

Unlike in other list-based systems, the way these seats are awarded depends crucially on how the candidates performed in the constituencies. With the exception of the party leader, who – if unsuccessful first time around – is automatically allocated the first PMP seat secured by that Leader's Party. All the other PMP seats will end up being awarded to those candidates who scored highest in the first-past-the-post part of the election (in other words, the strongest runners-up) depending on the support that their respective parties' level of support even when they lack sufficient strength in any particular constituency. Everything therefore depends on the number of votes each potential PMP candidate and his/her party secures.

Arguments in Support of TR

- Each voter is required to cast only **one ballot**
- No votes are **"wasted",** with most going on to secure at least some level of representation.
- Its PR element is relatively simple to understand and easy to operate
- All MPs would have to start off as constituency candidates, and all votes are worth fighting for even in "safe seats" because there is a potential prize also for coming second.
- It gives **minority views** the chance of a **voice** in parliament without giving them

undue influence, because the system is still weighted towards First-Past-The-Post.

Arguments against TR

- It creates **two "classes" of MPs (CMP and PMP)** However unlike in other such systems, most of the "Party" MPs would also have to rank at least second in their constituencies and therefore would continue to retain a close link with that constituency waiting for the next opportunity. The central duty of the CMP is to represent their constituency, that of the PMP is strengthening the Party in Parliament while preparing for the next round of elections.

- All existing constituency boundaries would have to be redrawn periodically (as the case is now) but more so to ensure similar and comparable sizes of electorate / number of voters in all constituencies. This is in line with the latest work by the Boundary Commission.

CHAPTER 2

APPLYING TOTAL REPRESENTATION TO THE HOUSE OF COMMONS

I believe the key to a well-functioning democracy with a truly representative Parliament lies in combining our established First Past The Post (FPTP) Constituency System with some small yet significant adjustments at the margin, based on the principle of Total Representation (TR).

The system

The proposed system would preserve the UK's constituency and electoral systems intact but add a limited, sensitively judged element of proportionality so as to mitigate the worst side-effects of the constituency system while avoiding the perils of a proportional representation system.

Under such a system, Constituency MPs (CMPs) would continue to be elected by the people in their constituencies and would represent the interests of all of them in Parliament. Voters would continue to vote for individual people, not just the Parties to which they belong. This important feature of our present constituency system in the UK, crucial as it is in terms of a well-functioning representative Parliamentary democracy, would be maintained.

As is well known, however, a first-past-the-post (FPTP) constituency system such as we have in the UK also has serious disadvantages. While the votes cast for the successful candidate are represented in Parliament, the rest of the votes (notably those cast for the unsuccessful candidates) are left unrepresented. In many constituencies, however, the numbers of votes cast for unsuccessful candidates are substantial. Taken together, they often exceed the number of votes cast for the successful candidate.

At a national level, moreover, as a result of the way voters are divided between constituencies, the political Party which receives the most votes may not have the most MPs. More generally, the numbers of MPs of individual political Parties in the House of Commons may fail (and have indeed signally failed in recent years) to reflect the numbers of voters in the country as a whole who voted for the Parties concerned.

The TR-adjusted constituency system which this book proposes is based on the premise that, without sacrificing the constituency principle and with only minimal exceptions, every single vote cast in an election should be reflected in some representation in Parliament by contributing to the selection of Members of Parliament, directly or indirectly.

Systems of Proportional Representation (PR) do of course allow representation for all votes cast and give them equal weight (subject to any threshold levels which may be defined before any representation is permitted). But such systems, unlike the single-member constituency system, make no provision for a direct link between members of the electorate and their individual representatives in Parliament and make it difficult for regionally-based Parties to secure any representation in Parliament. The link between local people and individual MPs is broken. Representation is effected instead at the aggregate level of the Party nationally. A further, serious issue with PR systems is that they encourage small political parties and splinter groups, resulting in weak coalition governments where such groups obtain disproportionate power and influence; and factional rather than national interests then take over.

The TR-adjusted constituency system is designed to combine, as far as possible, the positive elements of both systems in a hybrid solution. The direct link with the voter of the Constituency FPTP system would be combined with a sensitively-judged degree of proportionality stopping a long way short of pure Proportional Representation.

In order to implement the TR element, Parliament would have two classes of MP who would be equal in every respect save for the manner by which they are elected. One class would be the Constituency MPs (CMPs) who would be elected in each constituency on a FPTP basis, exactly as they are today. They would continue to fulfil their duties and obligations towards *all* their constituents, dealing with individual problems and grievances at regular meetings in the local MPs' offices (called *surgeries* in the UK) or addressing wider national issues in local public gatherings.

The other class of MP, Party MPs (PMPs), would be elected by pooling all the "wasted" votes cast for candidates in the constituencies and allocating quotas of PMP seats to individual Parties in proportion to the number of such "wasted" votes cast for their candidates across the country.

The PMP seats within the Party quotas would then be assigned to individual candidates of the Party concerned as follows. Before the election, each Party would have announced a list of all its constituency candidates. These Party lists might be arranged with the Party Leader at the top, followed by its strongest and most prominent candidates, in order to appeal to the electorate as a Party. Immediately after the Election, however, once the constituency results are declared, all the candidates elected as CMPs would drop off the Party lists, which would now consist of all the *unsuccessful* candidates re-arranged in accordance with the number of votes each of them had attracted in the constituency where he/she was competing. The candidates who had received the most votes would then be appointed as PMPs until the Party's allocated quota of PMPs had been reached. Individual PMPs too, therefore, would be directly elected by voters.

This procedure would provide added incentives for all candidates to fight for each vote in the constituencies, as this could be crucial in their being selected as PMPs if they failed to be elected as CMPs. Voters' incentives for tactical voting would likewise be much reduced.

Once selected, PMPs would be expected to discharge their Parliamentary duties like any other MP but would concentrate on serving the Party in Parliament, initiating new policies and bringing coherence to its legislative programmes while waiting to compete in the next election.

The relative numbers of CMPs and PMPs would be a significant issue. The more CMPs there are, the more closely the overall outcome would resemble that of the present Constituency FPTP system. The more PMPs there are, the more closely the overall outcome would resemble that of a PR system.

There is no perfect or correct ratio of CMPs to PMPs. The ratio would be a matter for judgment and political decision. The optimum ratio would be likely to vary between countries and over time.

In the UK, in the interests of avoiding unnecessary disruption the number of constituencies and CMPs could remain at 600, as presently planned, and that perhaps 75 PMPs could be added alongside, implying a CMP / PMP ratio of roughly 89:11. With a ratio such as this, Parliament would consist predominantly of CMPs, thus enabling a continuing high degree of government stability.

Other ratios would of course be possible. In the interests of caution, however, there is a case for having a relatively low number of PMPs, initially at least. By way of comparison, CMP / PMP ratios of 90:10 or 80:20 would mean having 67 PMPs or 150 PMPs, respectively, alongside the 600 CMPs.

The presence of a significant number of PMPs, along the lines suggested, would also help to ensure the existence in Parliament of a built-in opposition, backed by representation. Representatives of minority interests would be able to speak with authority on the floor of Parliament. Members of the majority (and therefore the government) Party and members of the minority opposition would draw their sovereign authority from the self-same body of voters in the constituencies. Both would directly represent the country's sovereign people.

Even in an extreme scenario where one Party had won *all* the constituency seats, opposition parties would win most of the PMP seats and therefore a substantial number of MPs overall. This built-in opposition within the system lies at the heart of any democracy based on genuine representation, countering in some degree the 'tyranny of the majority' that John Stuart Mill warned against.

Representing the opposition
It is important when talking about rights, freedoms and justice in an open society to bear in mind that all these concepts revolve around the idea of

effective opposition of one kind or another. The existence of such opposition is essential. Its legitimacy has to be recognized and safeguarded as an official part of representative democracy so that it may be heeded and respected by all sectors of society.

It is here that TR-adjustment of the constituency system scores highly. One of its great merits is the balance it would maintain in the results of elections between winners and losers. This is an important innovative element. Losers as well as winners would be more effectively represented than under either PR or Constituency systems. Under constituency FPTP, the big parties dominate and suppress the voices of the smaller parties and pressure groups. Under PR, small groups can keep a stranglehold on the big parties and, therefore, the government. The inbuilt balance in a TR-adjusted constituency system should go far towards rectifying both faults. The losers would become watch-dogs in the constituencies as well as in Parliament, thus preventing Government Party MPs, especially in safe seats, developing into an oligarchic establishment.

The concept of opposition in general, and political opposition in particular, is the kernel of an 'Open Society', as discussed in the famous book by the

Austrian Anglophile, Karl Popper[5]. The role of the opposition is not to put permanent blocks in the way the majority of a community wants to govern. Rather, it is the door through which changes may find their way to transform society. Its absence renders a society 'closed' and backward-looking. A political system should therefore contain such a kernel, institutionalised as an integral part of the structure. This kernel must have the freedom to grow or give way to others within its wider social context.

As the above implies, any political system for representative democracy should provide specifically for permanent representation for the opposition such as will enable it to fulfil its function. This has traditionally been, and needs to remain, a key feature of the UK's political system. The familiar concept of 'Her Majesty's Opposition' might look to outsiders like a quaint, contradictory expression of British eccentricity. In fact, it is an essential ingredient of the UK's tolerant constitutional arrangements based on representation. Under this arrangement, the Government of the country and the Opposition both represent the Sovereign people. We should, therefore, not visualise the concepts of majority

---

[5] *The Open Society and its Enemies*, by Karl Popper (1945)

and minority as two static, adversarial sections of the political structure. Rather, we should see them as parts of the same structural representation of the Sovereign people, stimulating each other in a permanent ebb and flow of movement and change.

More generally, democratic institutions need to be designed to accommodate changing views and circumstances as well as differences of view. This is what Popper's 'Open Society' is all about. Social changes and the constant process of adaptation to new circumstances need to be "open-ended." Without this, social malaise may occur, and society may fragment.

In my opinion, Total Representation could help in resolving such tensions by explicitly giving voices to minorities as well as the majority, losers as well as winners.

UK Constituency System and Israel's Proportional System

The strength of a democracy is not purely a function of its method of carrying out elections. However, close observation of two countries – Israel and the United Kingdom – over the past half-century has led me to the conclusion that such systems can make a substantial difference in persuading voters that engagement with politics is worthwhile.

In both countries, around one-third of electors are not exercising their right to vote. Flawed or outdated electoral models – even within a strong democratic framework – can lead to feelings of frustration with politics and voluntary self-disenfranchisement.

The United Kingdom is the classic example of a system which seeks to provide stability and strong government above all else. Its Constituency FPTP model has many advantages. In its pure form, however, it may (and often does) fail to reflect adequately the balance of opinion in the country and in particular the views of political minorities, who often feel they are being treated as outsiders.

Israel lies at the other end of the spectrum. Its pure form of Proportional Representation (PR) is, in theory, the fairest and most representative system in the world. In practice, however, Israeli politics has been bedevilled by instability, with minority parties able to hijack the agenda, bring down governments and distract attention from important national issues. Many people in Israel find this exasperating, but mostly they take the view that this is what has always been and nothing can be done about it. They have switched off.

Various proposals have of course been made at various times for developing hybrid systems to tackle the key issues of reasonable representation, wasted votes and stability. One of the best known of these is the Single Transferable Vote (STV) system. Typically, however, these systems sacrifice the powerful advantages of a constituency system, as well as being complicated, both in concept and in operation, and sensitive to the particular counting procedures chosen.

By-elections
If a CMP (Constituency MP) resigns or dies, a by-election would be held to replace him/her. The successful candidate, the first to pass the post, would win the vacant CMP seat by a simple majority. The rest of the votes would not count in by-elections.

If a PMP (Party MP) resigns or dies, he/she would be replaced by the (previously unsuccessful) Party candidate who had won the next most votes in the latest election.

Electing the Party Leaders

The methods for electing Party leaders which Parties have developed over the years, not least in the UK, constitute another serious fault-line in Representative Parliamentary Democracy, further (and to some extent unintentionally) deepening the troublesome disconnect between voters and Parties via their representatives in Parliament and deepening political disenchantment.

In keeping with the spirit of Representative Parliamentary Democracy and Total Representation discussed above, Party leaders should be elected using the transparent method outlined below. This method would remove the need for primaries and for defining which Party members have the right to vote for new Leaders, with all the associated turmoil and scope for abuse. It would reduce the influence of money in politics and eliminate a very common potential source of corruption and abuse.

Any MP would be eligible to stand in the leadership contest for his/her Party if openly sponsored by a minimum of (say) 10% of the total MPs of that Party in Parliament or in smaller Parties by (say) one-third or one-quarter of the total MPs of that Party.

The supervising, counting and checking of votes cast could be entrusted to a panel of elders of the Party or to a panel of independent arbiters such as retired judges. In the case of complaint by (say) 5% of the Party's MPs, the process of election could be appealed and scrutinised by the Electoral Commission, even though this would be an internal Party election.

Those voting in the leadership election would be all the candidates who had stood for the Party concerned in the previous general election, or by-election, whether or not they had been successful. The voters would therefore include MPs and non-MPs.

The individual MPs and unsuccessful candidates would not carry equal weight. Instead, each of them would cast the number of votes that they had actually won in the last election or by-election. If, for any reason, any of them should no longer be available to exercise this duty, the chairman of his/her local constituency party might be allowed to deputise in casting these votes.

With this method, the Party Leader would be elected **by proxy**, indirectly, by all the supporters who had actually voted for the Party at the last general election or by-election. The MPs and unsuccessful candidates casting the votes would be expected to represent their real, committed supporters, consulting them in advance, exactly as they do when they vote on legislation in Parliament.

This method would avoid conferring the right to vote for a Party Leader partly or exclusively on the Party's signed-up or paid-up members. In the UK, widespread concerns about the associated abuses and corruption would be removed. Signing-up or paying a Party subscription (typically very small) should not buy voting rights. It would no longer be possible for particular factions within the Party, or indeed for mischievous members of other Parties, to infiltrate the rank and file of Party membership so as to ensure election of their preferred candidate.

The proposed method would confer more legitimacy on the elected Party Leaders than existing methods. It would discourage unsuccessful leadership candidates from trying to undermine the duly elected Leader.

The method could be used to elect Party Leaders in any constituency-based electoral system, including our present Constituency FPTP system as well as a TR-adjusted system. It would not, of course, be possible under PR systems with no constituency basis.

For over 40 years I have been advocating this simple and transparent procedure for electing Party Leaders. As long ago as 4th November 1980, *The Times* published my simplified version on its letters page.

Some advantages of a TR-adjusted system

As discussed earlier, a TR-adjusted constituency system would have the great advantage of maintaining a more sensitive balance between winners and losers in elections than Constituency FPTP or PR systems can offer. It would engage the entire electorate and enable Parliament to represent all shades of opinion within a more truly representative Parliamentary democracy. Its introduction and implementation would help to restore people's flagging faith in the democratic process.

The proposed system would be simple, readily understood and easy to implement. It would avoid the complications of other hybrid systems that attempt to fuse together the constituency and proportional representation models.

The system would not require the complicated mathematical formulas that characterize PR systems based on Arithmetical Democracy. These started with Thomas Hare's proposals in the 1850s to 1870s for STV (Single Transferable Vote) but were followed by D'Hondt and dozens of others with more complicated formulas designed to express the broad principle of proportionality in a precisely specified manner. The trouble, or more precisely one trouble, with such systems is that they pass over the heads of ordinary people, turning Parliament and elections into a remote domain presided over by a *clever* ruling establishment. The TR-adjusted system would bring simplicity back to the electoral process and ensure the direct involvement of all the citizens in it.

The proposed system would encourage candidates to fight for every vote, even when they feel they may not have much chance of winning a particular seat. Unsuccessful constituency candidates would be heartened by the knowledge that they might end up as PMPs – if not in that same general election, then in a future one. Since all candidates would be competing for the positions of both CMP and PMP, high-calibre candidates of one Party would be encouraged to offer themselves, and persist in doing so, even in constituencies where overwhelming support was enjoyed by another rival party, as is the case in safe seats in the UK.

Under a TR-adjusted system, the centre of gravity of political life would spread throughout the whole country, with the constituency being the central area of competition. Constituents who feel disappointed with the performance of their candidate in a general election would typically have four or five years in which to prepare his/her replacement in the following general election. With political activities diffused around different parts of the country, central political parties would be obliged to sustain their platforms by engaging local communities through their party constituency organisations. The bond between the constituency voters and their chosen candidates would be kept alive and would probably survive even when a candidate failed to secure a CMP seat.

The introduction of a TR-adjusted system would encourage smaller Parties and factions to unite into wider political groupings. By their nature and composition, such larger Parties would become more representative coalitions of interests and ideologies. So the curse of fragile and unstable government coalitions that plagues PR systems would be moved away from Parliament and into the political Parties, where it would cause less disruption to government.

The proposed system would remove the need for the blocking thresholds often perceived as necessary under proportional systems to prevent the disintegration of Parliament into small Parties. It is hard to reconcile such blocking devices, depriving voters as they do of their right to representation, with a representative democracy. To be effective in preventing a multiplication of small Parties with power out of all proportion to their support within the electorate, the blocking percentage needs to be very high. In Turkey, for example, it is set at 10% of the electorate. The pressure then builds up over the years and results in widespread public disaffection that may cause the system to implode. With a smaller but still substantial blocking percentage of 5%, the largest Party in Germany was obliged for decades to depend on, and make major concessions to, the third-placed or fourth-placed Party.

A constituency system with TR-adjustments, on the other hand, would have a built-in blocking mechanism. Although the voices of smaller Parties would be heard through the proportional allocation of PMPs, the predominance of CMPs would mean that such minority voices would be less able to gain undue influence. PMPs would generally need many more votes than CMPs to gain a seat.

Bringing all shades of opinion within the tent of Parliament and allowing them unrestricted access to field candidates in the constituencies would blunt the edges of fundamentalist movements and draw politics away from the extremes towards the centre. In order to increase their chances, candidates in the constituencies would naturally direct their appeal towards the centre ground.

Differential weighting of electoral votes
One objection levelled against hybrid systems is that they give different weighting (ie. the number of electoral votes needed to elect) to different voter categories. In general, as already noted, many fewer votes would be needed to elect CMPs than to elect PMPs. There are, however, two particular considerations which justify this.

First, the different weighting is a compromise which would help to keep a balance between two often conflicting requirements of any system: representation and stability. Retention of the constituency system and CMPs would provide stability and representation at a personal level which the UK's present system has traditionally and successfully provided but which pure PR systems cannot offer. The addition of PMPs would ensure that all voters (with only limited exceptions) have some representation in Parliament and that the balance of Parties in Parliament does not depart too far from the balance of voters in the country, thus achieving a reasonable proportionality and addressing one of the potential problems of a pure constituency system.

As discussed earlier, the ratio between CMPs and PMPs would need to be discussed and decided according to the circumstances of each country. Second, voters who elect a candidate in the constituencies have voted for the candidate individually and not just for the Party to which he/she is affiliated. They have voted to elect this particular candidate to represent them in Parliament. It seems reasonable, therefore, that these electoral votes should carry rather more weight than votes which are pooled and given to Parties as a whole.

In an historical perspective, differential weighting of votes is not a new concept. As democracy has developed, different representational weight has been given to different classes, religious leaders, property-owners or groups commanding big followings. John Stuart Mill himself, the champion and proponent of total, universal, egalitarian franchise, toyed with the idea of giving different weighting to the educated classes. But the element of weighting in TR would reflect the need to achieve a workable, acceptable fusion between constituency and proportional systems, local and national perspectives, stability and representation. It would not, of course, be based on class, culture, ethnicity or ideology.

Simulations of PR and TR

The following two tables compare the actual results of the 2015 and 2010 General Elections with simulations of the results based on Pure Proportional Representation (PR) and two variations of Total Representation (TR).

Table 1

UK Election 2015

Seats actually won compared with simulations of seats won under pure PR and under TR (two variants)

System	Actual FPTP	Pure PR	TR 80:20	TR 90:10
CMPs/PMPs	na	na	520/130	585/65
Cons	331	240	290	311
Lab	232	198	223	226
UKIP	1	82	34	17
LD	8	51	25	17
SNP	56	31	45	50
Green	1	25	11	6
DUP	8	4	7	7
PC	3	4	3	4
SF	4	4	4	5
UUP	2	2	3	2
SDLP	3	2	3	3
Indep	1	0	1	1
Others	0	7	1	1
Totals:	650	650	650	650

Notes:
- Total seats (CMPs+PMPs) are constrained to 650 in both TR cases so as to facilitate comparisons
- For an overall majority, a party (or Coalition) would have needed 326 seats or more

Table 2

UK Election 2010

Seats actually won compared with simulations of seats won under pure PR and under TR (two variants)

System	Actual FPTP	Pure PR	TR 80:20	TR 90:10
CMPs/PMPs	na	na	520 /130	585/65
Cons	307	235	274	290
Lab	258	189	236	247
LD	57	150	93	74
UKIP	0	20	8	4
BNP	0	12	5	2
SNP	6	11	8	7
Green	1	6	3	2
SF	5	4	5	6
DUP	8	4	7	7
PC	3	4	3	4
SDLP	3	2	3	3
UCUNF	0	2	1	1
Eng Dem	0	1	1	0
Alliance	1	1	1	1
Independent	1	0	1	1
Others	0	9	1	1
Totals:	650	650	650	650

NOTES
- Total seats (CMPs+PMPs) are constrained to 650 in both TR cases so as to facilitate comparisons.
- For an overall majority, a Party (or Coalition) would have needed 326 seats or more.

CHAPTER 3

APPLYING TOTAL REPRESENTATION TO THE HOUSE OF LORDS

Introduction

This Chapter sets out the much-visited subject of how best to reform the House of Lords, with special reference to the role which the principle of Total Representation (TR) might play in electing members of the reformed House.

The need for a second Chamber

The first question, clearly, is: do we need a second chamber? The answer is an emphatic Yes.

The purpose of the House of Commons, as representatives of the people, all the people, is to legislate by proxy on their behalf and supervise the State's Executive branch, the Government. As the House of Commons has evolved in the last hundred years, however, it has become dominated by political Parties which are too often willing to put Party interests above national priorities. The Parties, with their Whips, have come to dominate the House of Commons, pushing it into constant adversarial confrontations, and the Legislature, and first arm of State, has become subordinated in large measure to the Executive, the Government.

These unwelcome developments have made the case for having a second Chamber more compelling than ever. Like many others, therefore, I believe that the House of Lords, suitably reformed, has a continuing and important role to play as a second, independent Revising Chamber which can ask the House of Commons to think again and has the power to delay, but not ultimately to frustrate, decisions of the House of Commons.

An elected second Chamber

To fulfill this role, and indeed to be genuinely part of a democratic Parliament at all, the House of Lords needs to represent the people, and therefore to be an elected House. A non-elected Parliament is almost a contradiction in terms. As Lord Strathclyde, then Leader of the Opposition in the Lords, wrote to me in a letter of 25th November 2003,

> *"For my part, I have a simple view. I think that in the 21st Century the political members of a House of Parliament should be elected directly by the people."*

On 4th October 2004 Lord Falconer, then Secretary of State and Lord Chancellor wrote to me :

> *"The Government's aim is to create a second chamber which fulfills a very important role within Parliament, as a revising chamber for legislation and as a body made representative of the nation."*

The reformed House should therefore not be made up of unelected hereditary peers and other peers whom Governments can appoint in order to assure themselves of a majority, thus frustrating the main purpose of such a House. Continuing to appoint Lords in this way, so as to duplicate the Commons, is bringing the House of Lords into dysfunction and eventually into disrepute.

Neither should members of the reformed House of Lords be entitled to remain members throughout their lives. On the contrary, members of the House should be elected by the people for a fixed term of years, perhaps six years, with sensitive arrangements for transition from the present membership.

As with the House of Commons, there would be considerable merit in using a system which combines Constituencies with Total Representation (TR) for electing members of the reformed House. Apart from being a good system in itself this would help to restore the long-lost link between the Lords and the electorate across the country.

The electoral system and other arrangements should be developed so as to provide maximum assurance that the reformed House does not become a replica of the House of Commons or another rubber-stamping subordinate of the Government of the day.

Later sections of this Chapter will return to these points.

Functions

I assume that a new Act of Reform would broadly confirm the existing functions of the House of Lords, as defined in the Parliament Acts of 1911 and 1949, including its power to propose changes to most legislation and delay its passage but not ultimately to frustrate the will of the Commons.

Membership

As already suggested, the reformed House of Lords would consist entirely of members elected by the people for fixed terms of years, and representing the people who have elected them, **with sensitive arrangements for transition from the present membership.**

Some commentators argue that we need to retain some appointed Lords to ensure the presence of experts. In my opinion, this is a spurious argument. The House of Lords was never intended to be a House of experts. Governments and Select Committees of both Houses can and frequently do draw on expert advice from outside. Parliaments exist democratically to represent the ordinary citizen, not to create oligarchies and establishments that further distance the representatives from the represented.

There are, however, two categories of people who have traditionally been members of the House of Lords and whose special status could if desired, be recognised, with suitable modifications, within the new arrangements. These are: Law Lords and Bishops.

The challenge would be to give these dignitaries, few in number, a special status within the new chamber without doing violence to the Montesquieu principle of separation of powers between the three arms of State – Legislature, Executive and Judiciary – and without sacrificing the principle that the new House of Lords should consist entirely of elected members.

The solution could lie in providing for a number of non-voting Judicial and Religious Assessors who would be allowed to participate actively in the deliberations of the new House of Lords and its Committees but would not have the right to vote.

The Judicial Assessors would preferably be members of the Judiciary with real and current Bench experience, so that a direct link between the sovereign people and the judiciary would be maintained. The Supreme Court might delegate a small number of judges from the practising Judiciary to sit in the Lords on this basis and contribute as appropriate to its deliberations for a certain limited period – say six years. After these six years, they would be rotated and replaced by others.

Similarly with Bishops and / or other religious leaders, the Queen as Sovereign could appoint a small number of these to sit as Assessors in the new House on a similar, non-voting basis, again for a period of six years, after which they too would be rotated.

Arrangements on these lines, though by no means essential, could neatly solve the problem of how to replace the Law Lords and Bishops, thus maintaining the *gravitas* of the second Chamber. Such arrangements could also help in the vital task of restoring social cohesion in the UK, which has been threatened by social and ideological trends from within and as a result of an unprecedented scale of immigration from without.

I would also see advantage in continuing to have within the House of Lords people with long experience of important areas of the public and private sectors.

The House of Commons now includes many young people who look at their membership of Parliament as a career. They have become professional MPs. In my opinion, however, membership of Parliament should not be a profession. The recent development of this practice has contributed to the chasm between citizens and the MPs they elect to represent them, who look at their membership as a job for life. It is only the enterprising among them who move on and use their parliamentary positions as launching-pads to

43

go forward into other careers, often more remunerative or more rewarding, in business, journalism or academia.

To avoid creating a similar problem in the new House of Lords, and to balance the two Houses as to age and experience, I would see a case for fixing the minimum age of members of the Lords at 40. This would help in attracting individuals with wide experience from a variety of backgrounds, some of whom at least would have already made their mark or their fortune and so would be able to devote the mature years of their lives to public service rather than building up new careers elsewhere.

There may also be a case for limiting the service of individual members of the reformed House of Lords to three or four six-year periods and introducing an upper age-limit of 75 or 80. This could help the new House to maintain its vitality and avoid inertia.

Elections to the new Chamber

As discussed earlier, I believe that a system combining Constituencies with Total Representation (TR) would work well for electing members of the reformed House of Lords as well as the House of Commons. How might such a system be applied in practice to the Lords?

Here, as in the Commons, there would be a range of options. The numbers should be seen as an illustrative guide, and not set in stone.

- The new House of Lords could have (say) 300 members.

- 200 of these could be Regional Lords (RLs), elected like Constituency MPs through a Constituency FPTP system, region by region.

- Each House of Lords Constituency or Electoral Region would consist of three contiguous constituencies out of the 600 House of Commons constituencies due to be introduced from 2018. This would remove the need for a whole new exercise by the Boundary Commissions to determine Lords Regions and would vastly simplify the ongoing tasks of organisation and administration. The UK already has far too many conflicting administrative geographies and boundaries which are a major source of waste and inefficiency.

- The remaining Members of the reformed Chamber (up to, say, 100) would be Party Lords (PLs). It would be a matter for decision how many of these there should be. If the chosen number were 100, that would mean a ratio of Regional to Party Lords of 67:33. The proportion of Party Lords would then be higher than those discussed earlier for Party MPs in the Commons, thereby giving a significantly higher weighting than in the Commons to "wasted" votes. This might, however, be considered appropriate for a more independent second Chamber with less Party whipping (see further below). It would significantly reduce the likelihood that any single Party in the reformed House of Lords would have an overall majority. It might also correct to some extent for the relatively low weighting of Party MPs (PMPs) envisaged for the Commons.

- As in the House of Commons, Party Lord quotas of seats would be allocated to individual Parties in proportion to their shares in the aggregate of "wasted" votes they had obtained, and the Party quotas of seats would then be allocated to the individual candidates within each Party who had personally won most seats in the election, in the same way as described for Party MPs in the House of Commons.

Provision for Independent or Cross-Bench Lords

Independent or "cross-bench" Peers have traditionally contributed much to the work of the House of Lords. It would be good to enable this tradition to continue.

To that end, I would hope that Parliament might agree to strengthen and codify an existing, un-codified tradition whereby all members of the House of Lords, whatever the Party banner may be under which they have been elected, are encouraged to assume a degree of independence, seeing their main allegiance as being to Queen (in accordance with the oath sworn by Members of both Houses of Parliament and the more recent House of Lords Code of Conduct) and acting in case of need according to their own consciences and judgments of the public interest rather than following Party lines. The Office of Party Whip should preferably be abolished, as should the central aisle, so as to convey that all members, once elected, become "cross-benchers" first and foremost.

Whether or not that can be achieved, one consequence which may still be seen as regrettable of an electoral system on the lines proposed, is that independent or "cross-bench" candidates who wish as a matter of principle to forswear affiliation or allegiance to any of the political Parties, would have a lesser chance of being elected than candidates who are so affiliated. Such candidates might include aspiring people with professional backgrounds or experience who could bring much value to the House.

Candidates of this kind, though they would lack the back-up support which Parties may provide, would in other respects have a similar chance with Party-affiliated candidates of being elected as *Regional* Lords, especially if there was a good public understanding of the different natures of the two Houses. They could stand in the regions as Independent Candidates.

Other things being equal, however, they would have no chance of winning seats as *Party* Lords when the "wasted" votes are allocated to Parties. So the electoral system could be seen as being biased against potentially excellent candidates who wish to forswear *any* Party affiliation or allegiance.

It might be necessary to accept this as being a consequence of having an elected House with good representation of the people.

Candidates wishing to run as independents could, however, improve their chances of winning Party Lord seats by teaming up or forming pre-alliances with other like-minded independents. Alternatively, they might be able to form a "strictly non-partisan" Party exclusively consisting of candidates who wish to forswear affiliation or allegiance to any of the political Parties and are committed to act and vote individually according to their consciences and perceptions of the public interest, drawing on their professional expertise and experience. That would be the Party's (sole) declared policy and position. Such a Party could even prove to be a significant force in the reformed House of Lords as well as helping the new House to attract professional candidates similar to those who have contributed so much as cross-benchers in the present House.

Constituency sizes and responsibilities

As already implied, an electoral system for the reformed House of Lords which combines Constituency and TR elements would require regions or constituencies to be defined.

Under the proposals already discussed, the reformed House would have only one-third as many Regional or Constituency Lords as there would be Constituency MPs in the Commons, representing only one-third as many regions or constituencies. Each House of Lords region or constituency would comprise three House of Commons constituencies.

This would not be a problem but rather a strength of the new system. Regional Lords would not have the same obligations which Constituency MPs have to maintain close contact at all time with their constituencies. They would not be obliged to set up "surgeries" similar to those of Constituency MPs. Their contacts would be more a matter of gauging the political temperatures of their regions and using these to inform the deliberations of the House. The roles of MPs and Lords would complement, rather than duplicate, each other. This in itself would add to the value of the Lords as a Revising Chamber.

Frequency of elections
As suggested earlier, members of the reformed House of Lords could be elected for terms of six years. Once the new system is up and running, elections for the whole House could take place every six years. This period would be fixed. Alternatively, elections for half the members could take place every three years. This period too would be fixed. In contrast with the Commons, the House of Lords would not be able to dissolve itself.

By-elections

If a Regional Lord dies or resigns, a by-election would be initiated and moved by an appropriate House Committee within two months of the death or resignation of the Lord concerned.

If a Party Lord dies or resigns, the next in line on the Party list of the preceding election – in other words, the previously unsuccessful Party candidate who had won the most votes in that election - would accede automatically.

Attendance and remuneration

Members of the House of Lords would be obliged to observe certain rules of attendance and would therefore be paid salaries and expenses. These would be fixed and revised from time to time by a Committee of the House of Commons, presided over by the Clerk of the Parliaments, to ensure neutrality and adequate consultation between the two Houses.

Expected results from such a system

It would not be especially useful to try to predict or simulate the results of the elections to the House of Lords under a system such as that proposed above. It is clear, however, that the composition of the reformed House of Lords will seldom, if ever, correspond exactly to that of the House of Commons.

There are two reasons for this. First, the relative weightings proposed for Regional Lords and Party Lords would differ from those for Constituency and Party MPs in the Commons. Second, the timing of elections to the two Houses is unlikely to coincide.

A further consideration is that the age and maturity of the new Lords (if the suggested minimum age-bar is implemented) would make them less dependent on their Parties and less inclined to bow to Party lines. The possible presence of Independent Lords, likewise on the basis discussed earlier, would similarly help to give the reformed House of Lords a different and distinctive voice.

The greater independence which the House of Lords would have as a result of all these factors should enhance the value of their revising function. The debates in the Lords would continue to command respect and attention by the House of Commons and the public at large.

Transitional arrangements
Finally, it would be important to implement the transition from the present House of Lords to a

wholly elected chamber in such a way as to relieve a possible constitutional limbo and smooth the path of reform.

One way of easing the process would be to start by electing just half the members of the reformed House through the new, TR-based constituency system. 100 Regional Lords and 50 Party Lords could be elected in this way for the first six-year term.

The remaining half of the initial members could be internally elected by the members of the present House. Following the precedent set by Tony Blair and Lord Cranborne when reducing the number of Hereditary Peers, members of the present House could elect from among themselves 150 Lords (both hereditary and life-peers) who would stay behind. These Members too could continue to serve for six years to ensure continuity and help initiate their new, elected counterparts.

Six years later, the first full national election of 300 Lords (200 Regional Lords and 100 Party Lords) would take place, producing a wholly elected chamber.

Alternatively, if it were decided that elections for half the members of the reformed House should take place every three years, the initial cohort of 150 internally elected peers could serve for three years and a national election for their successors (whose terms would last six years) could take place at that point.

The Clerk of the Parliaments could be tasked, with help from some members of both Houses, to decide which 100 Regional Constituencies chosen from north to south would be the first half to hold elections

A remaining question is what would best be done with the remaining Life Peers and Hereditary Peers who are not elected in this way but would like to continue as Members of the House.

There is a simple, creative answer. The political Parties, which choose, delegate, or appoint their candidates for election in the regional constituencies, could give priority to deserving sitting Peers within their Parties. These Peers would then have a chance of remaining in the reformed Chamber as Regional Lords or as Party Lords within the Party lists. Even if they failed to capture regional seats, their efforts would be rewarded if they score highly in the regions and thus propel themselves to the top of their Party lists within the TR system. Their chances of acceding to the posts of Party Lords would depend as much on their own reputations and canvassing efforts as on the support of their Parties.

Last, but not least, what about the titles of Lord and Baroness? It would be for Parliament to resolve whether members of the new House should be designated in this way. If the decision is that they should, then it would seem fitting that they should be allowed to retain their titles for life after their terms of office expire.

AFTERWORD

DEMOCRACY AT A CROSSROADS:
TR or PR

The ideas and the proposals in this book crystallised in my mind over the last half-century whilst I observed the shortcomings of democratic politics from two different perspectives, first in Israel and then in the UK. As a young man working at the Prime Minister's office in Israel in the early 1950's, my quest was not for electoral reform but rather a search for a way to integrate the disparate waves of Jewish immigrants coming to Israel from East and West and then to integrate them together with the Arabs in the country into one cohesive socio-political entity. It was then that I witnessed at close quarters the cracks which were starting to appear in Israel's political fabric as a result of "pure" Proportional Representation. Paradoxically "PR" served to deepen ethnic, religious and communal divisions rather than to heal them.

Britain faced a different challenge. I came to Britain in the early 1960's as a graduate at Oxford. Then I observed the political ripples created by the famous Rochdale, Torrington and Orpington bye-elections won by the Liberal Party. The Conservatives were getting tired and the Labour Party was not a credible alternative government. The idea of a Lib-Lab alliance was vigorously canvassed, though in vain.

That context and the political climate at the time convinced me that reform of the existing electoral system was needed to better reflect the wishes of all the electorate but equally that a pure first-past-the-post Proportional Representation System was not the answer. It seemed clear to me then that a combination of the best elements of the constituency-based and the PR systems had to be the better solution.

Meantime in Israel, Ben Gurion himself thought "PR" was weakening his Party's grip on the electorate and acted to replace Israel's pure PR system with the Westminster model. I thought then that if the Westminster model was coming under strain in Britain how could its replica in Israel function any better. So I sought a solution which could apply in both countries. **And that was how my idea of "TR" the Total Representation Electoral System, was born.**

At the heart of all electoral systems is the means to gauge the wishes of the voters, i.e. the people; to decide consensually how they want to govern themselves. This was at the root of the concept of Democracy which we inherited from ancient Greece onwards. While still at Oxford I examined the details of how our constituency based democracy originated and developed peacefully (in contrast to other countries in Europe) from the time of Cromwell and the Glorious Revolution onwards. The practical English, later on the British, managed to absorb all the shocks that other countries endured whilst keeping alive its **constituency based accountable political system.** Through the constituencies, democratic practices kept alive under the constant supervision of Parliament.

Of course social and political trends don't stand still. They are buffeted by changing circumstances. Still our system, based on the constituencies and their representation in parliament, has managed, so far, to absorb changes as they occurred. However we have to be aware that while our political institutions, anchored as they are in traditions (call it in a Quasi Constitution) with defined roles for the Constituencies, Parliament and even the Judiciary, are being tampered with by political parties and their leaders to such an extent that there is a danger that our system of government and governance might suddenly no longer be able to further absorb these continuous drastic changes causing our institutions, which served us well for three centuries, to crumble.

After leaving Oxford I went into business and travelled throughout the Far East when most of the countries there, including China, were undergoing transformations. My trading business took me also to Yugoslavia, as it was then, still united as one country in East Europe. Throughout my travels and contacts I observed closely how these countries were governed and what were the ideas which lay at the base of their integration as united political and cultural entities under going dramatic changes.

Some 20 years ago (at the age of 65) I retired from my trading business activities and concentrated on advising my son Michael on his investment business which he carried out from his offices in Sloane Square. That change afforded me free time and enabled me to resume my interest and direct involvement in political activities to promote my electoral system of TR. First in Israel where I initiated the change to TR (in Hebrew "Yitsug Shalem") with the help of Prof. Gideon Doron and Prof. Zeev Segal of the Tel Aviv University through a White Paper supported by very senior Members of the Knesset (the Israeli Parliament) which unfortunately, three times, had to be cancelled and re-tabled for a full debate in the Knesset due to sudden unscheduled general elections. In between I was appointed by the President of Israel as member of his Commission to review the political institutions in Israel. My proposals for my electoral system TR were accepted by the Commission with minor modifications in its final report,

In Britain too I promoted TR through the good offices of the Electoral Reform Society with the help of Dr Ken Ritchie its then Chief Executive who devoted a whole volume explaining and praising the TR system's advantages for the UK Parliament.

Meantime in many countries today outside of Britain the truth is that democracy has become more of a slogan than a political institution reflecting the reality of the governance of these countries. Coupled with PR as an electoral system where the winner takes all, most countries use the slogan of Democracy as a cover-up gloss to justify the rule of the numerical majority and to disregard the views of the minority. **This situation brings to mind the strong warning of John Stewart Mill of the danger of "the tyranny of the majority".**

Luckily the UK has so far escaped this situation. The reason for this is our accountable representative democracy which seems fortunately to still stand as a shining example of true democracy, as a government by the people for the people anchored in the constituencies from the Glorious Revolution onwards to the present day. In stark contrast to other systems ours still stands solid looking at the majority and minority as two essential alternating components of our political system. The minority party in the UK is called significantly "Her Majesty's Opposition". Put it in formal words: The Sovereign, ie. the Queen, transfers her governing political power to the whole of Parliament made up of its two parts: The Government and The Opposition. These symbolic terms gave rise to the emergence of our two-party system, each alternating in government. That was the norm when the Whigs and the Tories alternated. And when Labour rose to voting power they replaced the Whigs, the Liberal Party. **This binary political system of essentially a Two Party Duopoly lent solidity and stability to our political system** as it allowed the opposing two big parties in Parliament to transform themselves each into internal coalitions. A change to PR will shatter that stability in our governance.

In this context it is helpful to remember Professor Sir Roger Scruton way back in his book England – an Elegy (Chapter 8) where he observed:

'Nothing is better known about the English than the fact that they developed over the centuries a unique political system, and then planted it around the globe. Yet the nature of this system is widely misunderstood. The reason for this, I believe, is that the commentators have misidentified the fundamental principle on which the English constitution rested. Almost all popular historians and political analysts see the English system as an experiment in parliamentary democracy. In fact, however, the key notion was not democracy but representation, and it was as a means to represent the interest of the English people that we should understand the institutions of Parliament.'

Parliament historically was an assembly of representatives of various regions and interests who came together and sought common cause in order to reach agreements based on compromise that could be imposed on a willing people. Certainly, it was not designed to provide a tool which a majority could use to impose its will on a minority. This process of reaching a consensual compromise was helped by an inherent desire for fairness in the country at large, reflected by its representatives in Parliament. The concept of fairness and equity has always been, and remains, an overriding principle of British public life and one of the pillars on which even our judicial system rests.

The misunderstanding and confusion caused by the progressive de-coupling of democracy from its historical roots in this country of representation and equity has had a damaging effect on the practice of parliamentary democracy in many countries of non-English tradition that have adopted the Westminster model. This decoupling reflects an underlying social attitude. Where it occurred, those countries moved away from being open, dynamic societies and became rigid and ideologically orientated. A 51 per cent majority of votes cast or MPs elected has become the stamp of legitimacy for many such regimes around the world, ignoring the importance of catering for continuous and uninterrupted representation of the interests of the 49 per cent minority that the Westminster model started with and continued to nurture.

Unfortunately, another misunderstanding has recently crept even into this country as a result of theoretical and abstract indulgence by those who advocate Proportional Representation as the preferred route to what they perceive to be a more democratic political framework. The advocates of PR seem to overlook the essence of the constituency arrangement which, having evolved over the years, represents, through MPs and Lords, the interests of the people of the cities and the countryside vis-à-vis the central institutions of the State.

The status of these representatives has been gradually eroded by central political parties, to the point where MPs and newly appointed Life Peers today hardly relate to the regions or to the interests they purport to represent. Most of them have become party partisans. This process, that weakens the notion of representation, has contributed largely to the alienation of ordinary citizens. Gradually, the people have become disconnected from their formal or official representatives creating a mistrust of politicians and a blurring of lines between the legislature and the executive. Government and parliament have merged in the public perception and this has led to the clamour for referenda and for public inquiries presided over by independent judges. The holding of referenda is alien to the traditions of this country; political and constitutional issues have traditionally been dealt with by parliament as the sovereign voice of the people. So the new enthusiasm for referendums has been encroaching on the authority of Parliament and subverting Parliament. On the other hand, the seniority of the Legislature, where ultimate sovereignty should lie, is also being threatened by elevating the Judiciary to a dominant position in the public's perception. This is not the way representative democracy, or indeed any form of democracy, should work.

It is surprising why all these obvious and simple facts of our political system seem to be overlooked by those who want to engage in active politics. In some respects the Conservative Party seems to understand this situation a little better than others. They understood how to separate policies from reaching for power to implement them. They understood that politicking has to be exercised within the Constituencies first and then within Parliament. Their Party is composed of factions within the Party in Parliament. The Leader is elected and dismissed within the Party in Parliament and the all powerful 1922 Committee operates exclusively by its sitting MPs without interference of Party institutions outside Parliament.

The Labour Party, oddly though, doesn't seem to internalise these simple facts of our political life. They have forgotten that they came to power only after replacing the Liberals as the second Party in our binary duopoly system. Of course it is naïve to think that money can't buy you influence in either of the two dominant Parties (whether from Trade Unions or from wealthy supporters) but direct power and influence can only be obtained by success in gaining membership of the House of Commons through General Elections via the Constituencies. Electing the Leader of either Party by paid up Party supporters from outside Parliament sabotages our very political arrangements. And yet this is exactly what Labour did. This change, coupled with the clamour for pure PR will inevitably lead to Labour destroying itself and the political stability which we cherished for three centuries and already is leading to an alienation of the public towards the political class.

And with the recent inclusion in our society of new ethnic and religious groups and the emergence of the environmental movement, the feeling of alienation from the political class has been aggravated further resulting in the people demonstrating in Trafalgar Square and the streets to vent their frustration rather than through debate and dialogue by their representatives in Parliament.

Demonstrating is of course a fundamental political right. But when it becomes the main channel for dissent, taking over the role of parliamentary cut and thrust, it threatens democracy. It is a sign of political malaise when the delicate balance between the majority and the minority is disturbed. Perversely, it is then that the voices of a vocal and populist minority, seeking to exert their right to political expression, drown out the silent majority.

It has become imperative, therefore, to adjust our constitutional framework to the underlying new realities. The first-past-the-post system, as it operates today, is not helping to address these trends. It is this element of the constituency system which needs modifying or rather just tweaking. And it is "TR" The Total Representation Electoral System that I believe can provide that essential adjustment without harming the all important constituency based representation.

APPENDIX ONE

The EU Referendum Laid Bare
The Crisis in our Democracy
(31st August 2016)

Background and Context

To many, the results of the EU Referendum were unexpected and incomprehensible. In order to understand it we need to analyse it on two levels, examining two sets of facts. One set is to do with the specific circumstances that immediately preceded it. The other is to go deeper into its wider context and the background of the political changes that brought the alien concept of Referenda into our Representative Accountable Parliamentary Democracy. Both, Harold Wilson and David Cameron, used the beguiling institution of a referendum as a means to unite their Parties, unmindful of the damage that they would cause in undermining our very own Parliamentary Democracy.

Far from uniting their Parties both Governments and Oppositions managed to divide the country. The purpose of this essay is to show that the phenomenon of Referenda is a symptom of the crisis in our democracy. Whether we are in or out of the EU is no more than a matter of economic policy that needs to be reviewed and to change with circumstances. The impact of introducing Referenda has more enduring constitutional consequences on how we govern ourselves.

1.   For thousands of years, communities of humans sought social cohesion to enable them to live in peace together. Social cohesion is built on shared language, culture and moral values. This was at the root and the underlying conclusion of Aristotle's research into some 150 Poleis (City-States) which recommended that the population of a City State, Polis, ideally should be around 100,000 inhabitants to enable it to secure such lasting cohesion in order to govern itself consensually and peacefully. His pupil Alexander the Great shattered the idea and the cohesion it sought by creating an empire too vast and diverse to gel together. In the West today only Iceland and the Swiss Canton can be compared to Aristotle's Mediterranean Polis. All other countries have lost or are losing their internal cohesion, some fast, like the UK, others slower like the Scandinavian countries.

2.   Direct Democracy as the rule of the people by the people was possible and indeed was exercised in some Poleis, for example in ancient Athens, where the adult male population assembled at the city centre, the Agra, and decided on vital issues of state. But the consequences of wars and the influx of immigrations both created centrifugal forces that collided with the centripetal forces that held the society together. In Athens these centrifugal forces caused the erosion of direct democracy to the extent that Plato in his Republic looked to the likes of oligarchic and dictatorial Sparta to constitute his ideal society governed by the philosopher ruler. Dogma and

Ideology replaced evolutionary practicality. Ideology by definition is based on the past. Thankfully Plato's dream remained a dream, indeed a nightmare, from the past.

3. Skipping over 2000 years of political thinking the pragmatic English, (after 1707 the British) owing to historical circumstances re-created the concept of democracy and anchored it into the institution of a Representative Parliament. Avoiding dogmas and ideologies the British Genius let this new concept and institution evolve and adapt to the new circumstances that arose from time to time. The people and their rulers acted in tune if not always in harmony. This practical approach permeated all aspects of our lives and has been reflected even in our Judiciary. Our Judges over the years tempered the dictates of the cold rigid Law and balanced it in their verdicts with the underlying concept of equity and fairness. In that process judges in one way legislated from the Bench by creating Precedents that can guide but not dictate future verdicts. This legal procedure is often followed even today. In England the Montesquieu principle of the separation of the powers of the three Arms of the State (Legislative, Executive and Judiciary) emphasised in practice the coordination and not separation of these powers.

4. By the beginning of the 20th century our evolved system of a Parliamentary Representative Accountable Constituency System that guided us allowed our

democracy to continue to flourish and evolve. The two Houses of Parliament balanced each other as the House of Commons embedded within its ranks the Executive i.e. the Government and the Lords embedded the Judiciary, the Courts. Thus the three arms of the state, the Legislative, the Executive and the Judiciary moved in the same direction representing the British people while balancing each other through peaceful co-existence with their bases - The MPs represented the urban citizens and the rising bourgeoisie while the hereditary Lords represented the Shires. Thus it was taken for granted that the Constituency MP represented not his/her Party but all his/her Constituents while the Lords exercising responsibility spoke for the populations of their rural Estates and their surrounding countryside. Therefore Members of both Houses of Parliament were Representatives i.e representing the whole mix of the wider interests of their communities not the narrow interests of their Parties or their Classes. That produced a democratic edifice, the envy of the world.

5. However, at the beginning of the 20th Century all that balanced edifice began to crack and crumble and mindlessly our political establishments themselves began dismantling it brick by brick. This process was spurred by the deficiency in representation rooted in our Majoritarian FPTP Electoral System when winners take all, which is rigid and lacking the flexibility and elasticity to change with the times. Instead of reforming the House of Lords changing it to an elected chamber,

the Establishment of the Commons stripped it of its substantive authority eventually ending it being appointed by the very Establishment that it was meant to guide, balance and supervise. In the Commons, the MPs instead of being representatives were in effect converted into Party Delegates.

6. It started with the 1911 Parliament Act (with its follow up of 1949) when the power and responsibilities of the House of Lords were curtailed. Both coincided with the rise and rise of the trade unions and the Labour Party. What concerns us here is the effect on our constitutional arrangement not the merits or the reasons which brought it about. Politics became polarised and adversarial. The Press and the Media simplistically followed suit and projected each policy or argument into black and white, yes or no, or in new parlour "Binary"

7. Class war, not as in Karl Marx's lexicon but class as short for social grouping with shared interests, is at the root of evolution. Socio-economic classes are stacked on top of each other with the better-off at the top and the least fortunate at the bottom. For the purposes of research and statistics the ONS graded them into A, B, C1, C2, D and E. However what interests us here is not an objective grading but the subjective feeling of individuals as to which class they belong to and judge themselves deserving to belong to: the Upper, Middle or Lower Classes. As social conditions evolve the individual members of each class try to better their

position by climbing up and join the class above. The mechanism that blocks this natural social evolution brings about revolution or convulsion, in the past it was violent, today it is through the ballot box. If blocked it can lead or resort to violence. This has been enacted before our eyes today but we refuse to see it. As a result the strife for change is moving from Westminster to Trafalgar Square. The rise of Corbyn and his popular support as the leader of the Labour Party reflect the attempt of the rising lower middle class to take what they believe to be their natural right to participate in leading the country and shaping our society. This convulsion in our political system could have been absorbed and channelled through gradual changes as befit the traditional practicality that we are so famous for. However what obstructed this gradual smooth change that we needed was a fossilised Majoritarian electoral system which freezes the status quo and prevent natural and gradual changes.

8. Paradoxically the EU Referendum results, instead of leaving the Conservatives in disarray, resulted in Labour losing its opportunity to claim the victory. If the Labour leadership used its members and supporters to push for the Remain camp more vigorously and visibly, and with the Tory Party divided down the middle, the Labour Party could have claimed and indeed would have been credited with the result. Instead of its declared objective of Remain, the Labour leadership were busy fighting a class war with the Tories instead of leading the Remain factions of all parties. The EU

Referendum results are deepening the rifts within the Labour Party and causing a crisis in our democracy that the results of the 2015 Elections had left exposed, weak, precarious and vulnerable.

9.   It is interesting to contrast today's Labour Party leadership contest with that of 1980 following the resignation of James Callaghan. Callaghan who was Prime Minister from 1976 to 1979 and had stayed on as leader of the Labour Party for eighteen months in order to oversee an orderly transition to his favoured successor, Denis Healey, over his own deputy Michael Foot. (Contrast the behaviour of Callaghan with that of Miliband and compare the instant departure of the latter with the orderly withdrawal of Michael Howard after his defeat.) However, during that period the party had become bogged down in internal arguments about its procedures and future direction. (Plus ca change etc !) Initially, the candidates were thought likely to be Denis Healey, Peter Shore and John Silkin, but Michael Foot was persuaded to stand by left-wingers who believed that only he could defeat Healey (not defeat the Tories!) This was the last leadership election to be conducted amongst Members of Parliament only; an Electoral College was subsequently introduced for future contests. That procedure paved the way for Corbyn now to ignore the elected Labour MPs and to appeal over their heads to the wider membership in order to stay in power and lead the new wave that engulfs the Labour Party pushing politics to spill over

from Westminster Hall into Trafalgar Square with all the consequences that will ensue.

10. We must not take the Corbyn phenomenon lightly. The trend and the sentiments of many alienated young people are with him. When assessing his support we must remember that the overall percentages of turnouts in recent General Elections left one third who chose not to vote. How many of this third might support Corbyn and make a difference? The shift from moving the direct responsibility from Labour MPs to a college of voters for the leadership of Labour has in effect moved the centre of gravity from Parliament to the outside paid membership. Clearly the British genius of compromise that managed to keep all dissents within the tent of Parliament has deserted it.

11. The elected Labour MPs in the Commons have misjudged the mood of their young supporters in the country. Evidently in their judgment and indeed that of many political commentators Corbyn did not measure up to his new role. However With Labour now torn between Left and Right wings it needs an Attlee now to mediate between "Erbert and Erni !!" Hilary Benn could have fulfilled that role but he hastily messed it and missed it. Unless an Attlee emerges quickly the prospect of preserving unity in their Party will be difficult to achieve. Our concern here should be the enormous impact this is going to have on our Representative Parliamentary Democracy. We must not let any dissent group to take over and replace the

exclusive role of the electorate in choosing the leaderships of political parties in parliament.

12. To avoid such a situation, way back on 4 Nov 1980 I published a letter in The Times detailing a new transparent and democratic method to elect Party Leaders. I quote it hereunder in full for its relevance today. If my method were used for electing the Labour Leader then, and now, it could have avoided the turmoil that is convulsing the Labour Party on this very issue.

The Times, 4th November 1980
Electing Labour's leader
From: Mr. A. Nathan

Sir, The election of the leader of the Labour Party is of concern not only to the party itself but to all of us who value democracy in this country. May I suggest through your columns the following method of election hoping to test its merits by the reasons of your readers:

1. The leader is to be elected by Labour candidates of the last general election, ie by present Labour MPs together with all Labour candidates who failed to be elected.
2. The present procedure is to be maintained except for substituting the secret ballot by an open ballot.
3. Each elector casts the number of votes he or she officially obtained in the last general election as his or her votes for the leader.

In this method the leader is elected by all citizens who voted for Labour candidates, and therefore for the Labour Party, in the general election casting their votes by proxy.

That this method is both democratic and fair is self-evident and therefore any elaboration is superfluous.

Yours faithfully,
A. NATHAN
9 Highbury Road, SW19.
October 31.

Events leading to the EU Referendum

13. Blair started the process of shaking and undermining the UK Union. Exploiting the Pathological hatred of the Lairds, the absentee land owners identified with the Conservatives, Blair, anxious to perpetuate the dominance of Labour in Scotland as a cushion for its position in Westminster, revived the nationalist institution of the Scottish Parliament. Once he started it, and erected a monument of a building to house it, the genie slipped out of the bottle. Following the untimely death of Donald Dewar, the moderate safe hands, the Scottish ultra nationalists started their campaign to replace Labour as the dominant Party as a first step. The clamour for Independence was the clarion call and devolution became the vehicle to renege on the 1707 Contract of the Union. No one seemed to bother with analysing the results of the defective Electoral Mixed System on the

three Scottish elections results that followed which pointed the way to the ascendency of the SNP.

14.   Without any regard to the bigger partner, the combined English Welsh and Northern Irish of the Union, nor to all the Scots living south of the border in the UK, David Cameron agreed to hold a referendum restricting it to the those living in Scotland alone. He was wrongly relying on Labour in Scotland to deliver. But that was at the time when Ed Miliband was losing credibility and grip on his Party in Scotland casting doubt on his leadership in the country. David Cameron gambled on the future of the Union. His late realization of the possibility of losing the referendum resulted in Cameron showering the SNP with promises which later on he lived to regret. The results of 55/45 sounded good on the face of it when in fact they reflected the strength of the SNP who adroitly followed them by incrementally inching forward towards the ultimate objective of an Independent Scotland while meantime displacing Labour as the dominant Party.

15.   In contrast when Harold Wilson at the time opted for a referendum on the restricted objective of joining the Common Market the country was not divided and there was a genuine desire by all the Parties to ascertain the wishes of the people. We all thought that was a "one off" exercise in democracy not making it a new habit.   It is then that Harold Wilson announced his "Yes" recommendation supported by leading Cabinet colleagues   which he announced and defended. Still

even that in fact undermined the authority of Parliament. Clement Freud decided to ask his constituency how did they want him to vote following the debate in Parliament and he was told by some constituents : "Why are you asking us? after all we voted for you to vote for us." How wise those voices were.

16. It is here that David Cameron went disastrously wrong. Not having learnt the lesson of the Scottish Referendum he plunged into the new EU Referendum instead of waiting to 2017 as he promised because he was sure it was a walk-over. He wanted to finish it before the German and French Elections and get on with fulfilling his Manifesto while Osborne was succeeding in cutting the deficit and getting ready for the succession. In fact if he waited for the new Governments of France and Germany post their elections he could probably have squeezed better terms.

17. All over the world government leaders want to perpetuate their rules and secure their legacies by fair means or foul. The USA is the one country that protected its leader constitutionally from this character defect by restricting the Presidency to two terms of 8 years. In fairness David Cameron learning the lessons of Thatcher and Blair announced that he was not going to run for a third term. But he was overtaken and overwhelmed by events of his own making.

18. Philosophers and political thinkers over the ages were puzzled and tried to understand how people are swayed between Reason and Emotion. The root of Reason based on logic is in our human nature. We are born with it. Emotion on the other hand is in our acquired culture. We are tossed about between Reason and Emotion or between Nature and Nurture. Our emotional responses push aside our reasoned arguments. Between reason and emotion the latter wins. Durkheim, Freud and especially his nephew Bernays understood and explained this to us. And that was how the Public Relations Industry "PR" and packaging took off and took over insidiously and subliminally and controlled our responses.

19. So how is this question relevant to our argument? The answer is that while the Leavers played on the emotional fear of immigration, the Remainers concentrated their efforts on the reasoned economic benefits. So we the voters were tossed about between Reason and Emotion. The emotional responses of the majority pushed aside the economic reasoned insights in favour of the emotional responses of the immigration. Between reason and emotion the latter won.

So what now?
20. In the midst of this turmoil we need stability and first and foremost in order to avoid widening cracks in our democratic institutions and help us to face the consequences of what Brexit could throw at us. And so

while the Government will have to deal with the nitty gritty of Brexit we need to reach to new ideas and policies that will help to adjust our institutions and avoid in particular the break up of the UK in the process. May be instead of the Iron Lady and the Ice Lady we need to hark back for inspiration to Labour's Red Queen and her call "In Place of Strife" to repair and adjust our fracturing institutions.

21. There are in the public domain some solutions that could constructively and positively reform our political system to avoid a Class War and bring our electorate from Trafalgar Square back into Westminster Hall. Bewildered Edmond Burk's first reaction to the French Revolution in 1789 was to condemn it. Why could not those fiery French learn from our Glorious Revolution! Since those days our politics were conducted gloriously in evolutionary steps going along with the grain of our political cool temperament. It is in that spirit that our steps we take now have to be in response to the political chaos in which we find ourselves highlighted equally in their impact by the 2015 Elections and the 2016 Brexit

22.   The Referendum Results were fairly balanced 52/48. It will be advisable in dealing with the Brexit to remember this. True democracy takes into account the minority side of the equation, and more so as the difference between Leavers and Remainers is very small. The crisis in our democracy that the conduct of both Remainers and Leavers exposed reflected the

underlying more worrying division in our society as reflected by the electorate in 2015.

23.   Skipping over all the minutiae of statistics that many commentators and academics are so fond of and engrossed in, here are two glaring numbers from the 2015 results that tell all : UKIP's 3,881,1129 votes sent one MP to the Commons, the Lib-Dems with 2,415,888 managed 8 MPs. Compare and contrast these with 1,454,436 SNP votes securing 56 MPs!! The analysis of the other Parties demonstrates clearly the widening crack in our Electoral System of FPTP.

Solutions through Evolution not Revolution

24.   The ambitious response to change to a pure PR System proved to gain neither traction nor consensus. In fact if succeeded it would have created even more instability So let us resort to the simple, practical and pragmatic TR The Total Representation Electoral System which in essence can tweak the same FPTP without an upheaval. The details of TR are in the public domain advocated and analysed succinctly by Dr Ken Ritchie in his excellent book "Fixing our Broken Democracy – The Case for Total Representation"

25.   Basically TR is the fusion of FPTP Constituency System with PR in the proportion of 80:20 or say 500:100 simply through the use of one ballot. Once it is explained it can prove to be possible even for the present House of Commons to approve its introduction by simple majority to be followed by an Inter Party Committee to deal with agreeing the details of its

application. That is the first and most urgent step in order to restore to the House of Commons its prerogative to represent all strands of political aspirations of the electorate.

26. It is also an opportune time as the Boundary Commission is trying to adjust the number of voters in the constituencies to as equal number of voters in each to eliminate the big disparity between them. So instead of reducing the number of constituencies to 600 as proposed why not reduce that number to 500 MPs introducing TR at the same time by creating 100 Party MPs. The result will be 500 MPs from the constituencies elected by the Majoritarian FPTP as is the case now and 100 Party Members of Parliament "PMPs" elected by the combined number of votes lost in the same 500 Constituencies who did not succeed to secure any representation in Parliament. In this way the 600 MPs of House of Commons will still have the same proposed number of 600 using a combination of the FPTP and Proportional Representation "PR" in the ratio of 500 to 100.

27. The second step is to restore to Parliament its representative power by replacing the present appointed House of Lords with a smaller elected Revising House of 300 Members without infringing on the ultimate authority of the House of Commons. Any one of the present Lords can offer himself/herself as candidate for election for the new House.
28. My detailed proposals for a New House of Lords are based on totally elected 300 Lords in two stages.

The first stage is to select 150 from amongst the present lords on the lines of the Blair/Cranborne procedure of 1998. These "stay behind Lords" will supervise and guide the election of the first batch of 150 newly Elected Lords under the Electoral System of Total Representation, TR. After say 5 years the stay behind Lords will resign and will be replaced by the second batch of 150 Elected Lords. In this way continuity is maintained and the present functions of the House of Lords preserved. Full details of the purpose and procedure are contained in my Website. www.aharonnathan.com or just Google: Aharon Nathan on the House of Lords.

29. The third step is for the Parties to adopt the simple method of electing their Party Leaders as described in my letter to the Times of 4 Nov 1980 above. Such a Leader is to lead the elected MPs of that party in the Commons. That does not preclude electing a president or chairman to a party or movement outside the Commons that includes within its ranks the elected members of a Party in Parliament.

The above three steps can transform our political system gently and peacefully avoiding strife and upheavals by bringing the elected MPs and the elected Lords inside the tent of our accountable Parliament to represent and guard the wishes of all our electorate.

Aharon Nathan, Wimbledon, August 2016

APPENDIX TWO

The Binary of our Politics
The obstacle to a new Centrist Party
(20th April 2018)

1. The analysis of the results of the elections of 2010, 2015 and 2017 show a clear tendency of the voters to revert to a pure binary choice: yes/no, either/or. This tendency is not new as it is inherent in our system of government which combines the constituency system with a majoritarian first-past-the-post (FPTP) electoral procedure. It aims to create two political parties alternating in government; and that was how it worked for the last few centuries. This back to basics, back to a binary electoral choice, was reawakened and revitalised by the effect of the last two Referenda where a straight yes or no was required to determine the results. So, while before it had become easier for a third party like the Lib-Dems to grow, it once again became more difficult in the new electoral climate where there is no space for a third party unless it can replace one of the two incumbents. A new Party will take ages before it can achieve anywhere near to what the Lib-Dems achieved before it blew it up through arrogance and the euphoria of joining the Coalition in 2010.

2. When the two political parties: the Tories and the Whigs dominated parliament in the 19th century, their MPs and Lords came from similar backgrounds. Although generally Tories were rooted in land and

inheritance while the Whigs were merchants and professionals, their division was based on interests and policies not on social classes. One could say they merged into one Social Class. Their young attended the same private schools and aspired to serve in the army, the clergy and the colonies. In Parliament, although the two were divided in name and aim, there was no problem moving between the two. Gladstone started as Tory then he moved to lead the Whigs. Churchill started as Tory moved to the Whigs and returned to the Tories. They were all connected to different parts of the country through their constituencies. All that changed however with the advent of the Labour Party representing the working classes. Social Classing surfaced as the prime differentiation between parties and personal parliamentary representation gave way to party delegation. The Party took away the freedom of the individual member of parliament and transferred it to the party. The barriers between parties became rigid. The concept of Disraeli's one nation aspiration disappeared from our political canvass. Ideologies replaced national interests, delegation replaced representation and rigidity pushed aside flexible practicality. This situation is alien to our national tradition of fairness and pragmatism which characterised the genius of the people of this country.

3. Therefore we must not be surprised at the recent polarisation of political opinions between the extreme Left of Labour and extreme Right of the Tories resulting in a lot of recent talk in the media about

starting a new Centrist Party. As explained it is not easy to start a new political party which would take maybe two or three election cycles just to establish credibility. Moreover, it will be very difficult to attract sitting MPs to move their allegiances after years of loyalty and service. But above all in our present political and electoral system based on the constituency determining one victor there is no place for a third party. Under the Constituency FPTP System a new Party has to replace one of the two main Parties to survive. Otherwise it stays as a pressure group. In the early 20th century Labour displaced the Whigs. Towards the end of the Century the merger of the Labour Right with the Liberal Party breathed life into it with a hope of replacing Labour. Tony Blair saved Labour by reincarnating it into New Labour. That was made possible because it followed the earlier weakening of the two wings of the original Lib-Dem Party with the Two Davids (Steele and Owen) pulling in two directions that rendered it too weak to challenge the one or the other main Parties. Its revival at the end joining the Conservatives in Coalition blew its chance to become a viable main party. Charles Kennedy, the only Lib-Dem MP who voted against joining the Coalition understood that joining a main Party would lose its chance to replace either party. The last blow came about when they fought a hopeless Referendum campaign to replace FPTP with a faulty AV against the declared position of their Conservative partners.

4. Let us now consider also the anomaly of the recent elections results, e.g in the 2015 Election: 1,157,613 Green votes gaining one MP or 3,681,129 UKIP votes gaining one MP or even the Lib-Dems 2,415,888 gaining 8 MPs i.e. a total of 7,254,630 votes gaining just 10 MPs while 1,454,436 SNP gained 56 MPs! This is an affront to common sense and an insult to our concept of democracy. So with the considerable vote losses of the Lib-Dems, the Greens and almost the disappearance of UKIP there is little possibility of creating a new Centrist Party to challenge the one or the other of the incumbent parties under FPTP voting. But even if there is, pending that possibility, there is an urgent need to at least create a Movement that will give voice and hope to those 7-8 million fluid voters/dissenters of these three parties plus a similar number of voters who gave up voting altogether amongst the electorate in safe constituencies.

5. However another question pops up: why should the advocates of a new Centrist Party resort to the use of a sledge hammer when a screw driver can do the trick. All what they (and may be others like-minded) need to do is to canvass and create a national drive to tweak our electoral system and modify it to make a limited room for parliamentary participation for those dissenting floating voters left hanging in the air.

6. Such a tweak has been available in the public domain for the last 20 years and it needs to be dusted down and brought to the attention of the media, the political

leaderships and to all who care about our democracy. This is the innovative and simple system of TR Total Representation which gently modifies our present electoral procedure. TR is an Electoral System that fuses our present Constituency FPTP with a small dose of PR Proportional Representation. TR gives vent to the frustration and a temporary home in Parliament for those who do not support either the Conservatives or Labour and enables them to join together to build an alternative party with a view to potentially replacing one or other of the two main parties.

Aharon Nathan, Wimbledon, April 2018

APPENDIX THREE

IS THE UNITED KINGDOM BREAKING UP
The West Lothian Question
(31st October 2014)

1. The issue of **English votes for English laws**, commonly known as the **West Lothian Question**, refers to whether MPs from Scotland, Wales and Northern Ireland, sitting in the House of Commons of the United Kingdom, should be able to vote on matters that affect England only. The Devolution in Scotland highlighted this problem and put the question in focus owing to the significant number of MPs involved. The Scottish electoral system, AMS, devised specifically for Scotland was decided without due consideration to its consequences. It was an example of how a political party, Labour here, decided on measures which looked like benefitting that party at the time overlooking the wider public interest. That decision came to haunt Labour now.

2. Way back in my book on TR Total Representation published under the auspices of the ERS in 2009, I analysed in Chapter 7 the faults and consequences of AMS as applied to Scotland comparing it with TR (Total Representation Electoral System) My analysis was based on the actual results of the Scottish elections of 1999, 2003 and 2007. AMS is intended to reflect the

voting preferences of the electorate in a more representative manner than the Westminster model, retaining the best features of FPTP – direct though limited accountability – while introducing proportionality between parties through party list regional voting. So Scottish electors each has two votes: one to elect 73 Constituency Members of Parliament, using FPTP; and another vote to elect 56 Regional Members, using Proportional Representation "PR". **Broadly speaking, the percentage of votes obtained by the parties in the list vote (for Regional Members) determines their overall number of representatives;** these party lists are used to top up the FPTP seats to the required number. So if a party has won two seats in the Constituencies but its results in the Regional vote give it a proportion equivalent to five seats, the first three candidates on its list are elected in addition, and it ends up with five MSPs (Members of the Scottish Parliament). **Therefore in practice the component of PR in the AMS is the dominant and determining element.**

3. In comparison Total Representation TR is an electoral system based on the premise that every single vote cast in an election has to end up with representation in parliament directly or indirectly. It avoids the most serious defect of the first-past-the-post system, under which votes cast for the successful candidate are represented while all the rest of the votes cast for the unsuccessful candidate are are discarded and left unrepresented. Under TR these unrepresented

votes are totalled and distributed to the Parties of the Candidates (in proportion to their contribution to this Total) to elect Party Members of Parliament (PMP) Therefore TR offers a solution by fusing the positive elements of both systems FPTP and PR in one ballot one vote. And back to Scotland, **the following three paragraphs 4, 5, 6 are quotations from that Chapter 7** based on analysis in the tables provided of the actual results of Scottish Elections of 1999, 2003, and 2007:

4. **Here is what I wrote in Ch 7 in 2009**: *"In my view, giving voters two ballots is potentially dangerous and destabilising. My reason for saying this is that it tends to make people think in two different directions – and the system can become a playground for machination and manipulation by professional politicians and their public relations advisers."* and another quote *"A close examination of the results shows why the system is likely to become unviable. It is important to bear in mind when reading it that the calculations of the Regional seats are not based on simple straightforward conversion of percentages into seats to determine the resulting number of Regional representatives for each party. The calculation simply determines the topping-up requirements. That is why, for example, you find that (in 2007) almost equal percentages of votes of 29.1 and 31.0 for Labour and the Scottish National Party result in them winning 9 and 26 Regional seats respectively! The idea is to compensate the latter for its lack of success in the constituencies"*

5. *"Before the (2007) Scottish General Election, it was expected by the UK government that Labour, which was thought to be the most supported party, would win a majority. In fact, the desire of both the Labour government in London and the Labour Party in Scotland was to frustrate the efforts of the Scottish National Party to promote its platform of independence, and to show through the outcome of the election that the nationalists were in the minority and that Scotland did not want to break away. But close scrutiny of the results of 2007 show how AMS, the Additional Member System, subverted the results, and how a determined nationalist party,* **riding on a strong, emotional platform of independence**, *managed to overtake among the electorate the hitherto-more-supported Labour Party's objective of staying within the Union. The results of the Constituency votes compared with those for the Regional List votes already show the manipulation of the votes between the two ballots.* **Eventually AMS will break down**. *It was obvious that sooner or later the voters will split their votes in order to push forward the fortunes of sectional interests of minority parties – that is, unless the Scottish nationalists succeed in seceding from the Union. But that will be a different ball game."*

6. *"To examine the results of 1999, 2003 and 2007 meaningfully, one needs to compare the results of each participant party, and especially the way its voters split their votes in different directions. This comparison is especially significant when one sees that this split*

occurred in a big way among those who cast their Constituency ballots for the Liberal Democrats and the Conservatives and others – but not among those who voted for the two big warring blocks: Labour and the SNP. **The final results show the power of emotional, negative protest rather than rational opposition.** *A basis like this is bound to cause the system to fail sooner or later, sending the authorities back to the drawing board. A detailed examination of the actual results , reveals how – over three general elections – the Scottish Nationalists inched their way to the top. Their dip in the middle served to spur the voters of the other parties on to support them through the Regional votes to attain their objective of independence."* End Quotes.

7. All this occurred also, of course, because the Scottish National Party was better led and more organised at campaigning in 2007 than in 2003, and the demand for a non-Labour government was greater. In 2003, a large number of smaller parties, notably the Greens and the SSP, were elected, mostly from the List part of the ballot. It was in that election that the difference between constituency and list voting was more apparent and most significant, while in 1999 and 2007 there was a less of a gap between the two.

8. Indeed the faulty Scottish Electoral System led directly to the recent Referendum in Scotland and the chaos in the Westminster Parliament that unless dealt with wisely and quickly would be certain to lead to the

break up of the United Kingdom irrespective of the results of the recent referendum and not withstanding the result of 55% rejecting independence. And with the recent disintegration of Labour in Scotland its votes in the next general elections for Westminster could be overtaken by those of the SNP. We could then find Westminster dominated by a reinvigorated SNP as a powerful minority party side by side with the Lib-Dems and force the Conservative or Labour to play to its tunes. Therefore unless a proper response to the West Lothian Question is addressed now Scotland will become an independent country and the United Kingdom will be broken up.

9. Meanwhile Politics in the UK in all its aspects and institutions stand today under big question marks. The political establishment and the political institutions in the country have become the object of distrust and even derision in the eyes of the public. Westminster Palace has become the symbol of a historical fossil. Democracy itself is in a state of disarray. The political leaderships are in confusion. What are the answers? To create new parliaments for the regions? To abolish the House of Lords and replace it with a Senate? To leave the EU? These questions need to be settled by the people, the ultimate Sovereign. But we don't live in ancient Athens where we can all assemble at the Agra, vote and decide on our needs and our future. We are not Swiss either who grew up for centuries exercising their democracy through the practice of referenda in all levels of their politics, Communal, Cantonal and

Federal. Shaped by our own historical circumstances we elect representatives to think and decide for us. Unfortunately today there is a disconnect between us, the people, and our representatives, the MPs and the Lords. The fault lies in our outdated Electoral System of FPTP and the mutilations recently of the House of Lords. We need solutions for both based on our present circumstances and in tune with our traditions of practical commonsense and not on ideologies. The last thing we need now is the use of Referenda which is alien to our democratic traditions and therefore result in low participation and become easy to manipulate by vocal activists. That could certainly result in the subversion of the will of the British People the Sovereign.

10. So where are the solutions? And how to reconnect the voters, the people, to our politics? The answers to all those questions lie in reforming the tools of our Democracy which have become rusty and malfunctioning. And the biggest tool is our outdated electoral system that caused and gave rise to all these problems in the first place. But instead of understanding the basic faults of the system we tried to tinker with and patch up the problems derived from its malfunction.

11. **My solution has two prongs:** to replace our FPTP System with "TR" a modern electoral system that fuses in one ballot, one vote both the systems of FPTP and PR. And side by side to reform the House of Lords

converting it to an Elected Chamber while retaining its present revisory functions. I believe that the Smith Commission Recommendations are reversible. It would be advisable to the Welsh and Irish not to rush to clamour for devolution and independence. I would not be surprised that the May Elections could result in the SNP gaining more seats in the Commons. However I would not be surprised either that the SNP could end up later on after the Scottish Elections with no overall majority in Holyrood. The outcome of the implementations of the Smith Commission will highlight the enormous problems that the SNP has created to the Scottish people in Scotland, in England and in Europe. People cannot be fed with speeches, slogans and emotions.

12. As for England, the last thing we need is a multiplicity of regional parliaments. We have to distinguish between political aspirations and economic efficacy. Instead of devolving politics to the regions from London we must ensure economic prosperity there. We must not destroy in haste London as the great centre of finance serving the whole Union. London's role and function can only be in the field of finance. The North and the other regions are our industrial hinterland. Instead of transferring political power to them from the centre we must engage in injecting economic resources to create jobs and increase productivity. Instead of devolving political power to the regions we should revitalise our local governments and revive their glorious days before both the Conservative

and Labour denuded them of financial muscle and authority. Local taxation served good purposes in the past. We should revitalise the town halls that stood for local pride. It is then that a Councillor becomes a coveted office as important in the eyes of the public as an MP.

Aharon Nathan, Wimbledon, October 2014

.

Printed in Great Britain
by Amazon